The Library of
NATIVE AMERICANS

# The Algonquian

## *of New York*

## David M. Oestreicher

The Rosen Publishing Group's
PowerKids Press™
New York

*This book is dedicated to the memory of my teacher, Marvin Rothman, a man of courage, warmth, and humor, whose ability to open the minds of both young and old made him the very best.*

The author would especially like to thank his Mahican and Lenape friends who shared with him their heritage over the years. Thanks are also due to Paul J. Oestreicher and James Rementer for comments on the manuscript.

Published in 2003 by The Rosen Publishing Group, Inc.
29 East 21st Street, New York, NY 10010

Copyright © 2003 by The Rosen Publishing Group, Inc.

Photo and Illustration Credits: Cover and pp. 21, 27, courtesy of David Oestreicher, photographs by Cindy Reiman; p. 4 Erica Clendening; p. 6 courtesy of David Oestreicher; p. 9 © Jonathan Blair/CORBIS; p. 10 courtesy of Jeff Kalin, made by Jeff Kalin, photograph by Cindy Reiman; p. 12 courtesy of M.R. Harrington Collection, National Museum of the American Indian, Smithsonian Institution; pp. 15, 16, 19, 25, 43, 47, 50, 53 © Paul J. Oestreicher; pp. 22, 31 © Stephen Steinberg; p. 28 courtesy of Herbert C. Kraft and David M. Oestreicher, photograph by Cindy Reiman; p. 32 © Bettmann/CORBIS; p. 34 manuscript courtesy of Rare Book & Manuscript Library, University of Pennsylvania; p. 34 portrait courtesy of Transylvania University Library; p. 37, 41, 44 © CORBIS; p. 38 the Elliot Moses Collection, courtesy of the Moses family; p. 55 © John Running.

Book Design: Erica Clendening

Oestreicher, David M.
        The Algonquian of New York / by David M. Oestreicher.
            p. cm. — (The library of Native Americans)
        Summary: Describes the origins, history, and culture of the Native Americans who lived in and near what is now New York state, and whose languages were included in the Algonquian group, from prehistory to the present.
        Includes bibliographical references and index.
        ISBN 0-8239-6427-2
        1. Algonquian Indians—History—Juvenile literature  2. Algonquian Indians—Social life and customs—Juvenile literature. [1. Algonquian Indians. 2. Indians of North America—New York (State).] I. Title. II. Series.
E99.A349 O38 2002
974.7004'973—dc21

2002003761

*Manufactured in the United States of America*

*There are a variety of terminologies that have been employed when writing about Native Americans. There are sometimes differences between the original language used by a Native American group for certain names or vocabulary and the anglicized or modernized versions of such names or terms. Although this book contains terms that we feel will be most recognizable to our readership, there may also exist synonymous or native words that are preferred by certain speakers.*

# Contents

# THE ALGONQUIAN GROUPS OF THE NEW YORK AREA

New York

Vermont

Albany

Massachusetts

*MAHICAN*

Pennsylvania

Connecticut

*Munsee dialect of LENAPE*

Hudson River

New Jersey

New York City

*Unami dialect of LENAPE*

# One

## Introducing the New York Algonquians

Long before New York State was founded, before the tall buildings of New York City and Albany rose, and even before the first Dutch settlers arrived, this land was home to different groups of Native Americans. You can still find many traces of these first peoples in New York State in the beautiful place names that they left behind: Manhattan (which means "Island"), Rockaway ("Sandy Place"), Ossining ("Stony Place"), Taconic ("Cold River"), Wappinger (from *wapimgw*, "opossum"), and many others.

These names were left by groups of Native Americans called the Algonquians. There were many tribes of Algonquians, not only in New York but across much of North America. They spoke languages that were similar to each other, and even shared many of the same words.

The Lenape, who lived in the New York City area and the lower Hudson Valley, and the Mahican, who lived in the upper Hudson Valley and as far north as Lake Champlain, were among New York's Algonquian tribes. The Montauk, Shinnecock, and Unquachog of eastern Long Island were also Algonquians.

The Algonquians of New York and the surrounding states have been described by famous non-Indians. William Penn, the founder of the colony of Pennsylvania, admired the Lenape language and wrote: "I know not a Language spoken in Europe that hath words of

This map shows the homeland of the many Algonquian tribes.

Why do we call the Lenape, Mahican, and others "Algonquians" if they were different tribes? The word is taken from the name "Algonkin," an important tribe that lives in Canada north of the Saint Lawrence River. When European explorers first sailed into the Saint Lawrence River, the Algonkins were among the first native groups to meet them. As the Europeans continued to explore North America, they noticed that many tribes spoke languages similar to that of the Algonkins. They shared many of the same words and had a similar way of speaking, even though they could not always understand each other's languages very well. One French explorer, Baron de la Honton, realized that these tribes were all related and must have come from one ancestral tribe. Lahonton named all of them "Algonquians," a name we are still using for these groups today.

Algonquian languages are very different from the languages of other Native American groups, such as the Iroquois, the Sioux, or the Navajo. The Algonquians also occupied a larger area in North America than did any other family of Native American groups.

more sweetness or greatness . . . than theirs." The Mahicans are famous from James Fenimore Cooper's novel *The Last of the Mohicans*. Although this novel tells about the end of the Mahican tribe, in real life there are still Mahican Indians living today.

The Algonquians of New York have been written about, admired, and sometimes misunderstood. Who were these people? How did they get here? What happened to these people who first met the early settlers? What was their way of life like? How many of them are alive today, and where do they live now? What remains of their culture? What do they have to teach us, and what are they really like?

# The First Americans

Perhaps as early as 13,000 to 40,000 years ago—nobody really knows exactly how long—the first people crossed from Asia into the New World. The climate was far colder then than it is now. Glaciers, or vast sheets of ice, covered much of the continent.

For a long time many scientists believed that the earliest ancestors of Native Americans walked through corridors in the glaciers from Asia into America. Now other scientists are beginning to examine new evidence that people may have come to America even earlier in small boats, similar to the seal-skin kayaks used by the Eskimos.

We do not know what the first Americans called themselves or what languages they spoke. Scholars simply call them Paleo-Indians, a word that means "Ancient Indians" or "Ancient Native Americans."

Life for the Paleo-Indians was difficult. Unlike Native Americans of later times, Paleo-Indians did not know how to make clay pots or bows and arrows. They did not know about growing crops, and the climate would have been too cold for farming anyway.

To survive, men hunted large animals such as caribou, musk oxen, elk, and even the giant mammoths and mastodons. They hunted these animals with spears. This was very dangerous, and sometimes the hunters were killed. The Paleo-Indians probably also caught fish and hunted ducks and geese. Women made clothing, blankets and shelter from the animals' skins, and gathered berries and other edible wild plants to eat.

Scientists tell us that by about 12,000 years ago, the Paleo-Indians reached what is now New York State. Perhaps they were there even earlier than that, but so far no evidence has been found to show this.

# The Origin of the Algonquians

The way of the Paleo-Indians eventually came to an end. About 10,000 years ago, the climate began to warm. The glaciers—which then covered almost all of Canada—started to melt. As the ice sheets melted, the ocean began to rise. Long Island, which was once part of the mainland, became surrounded by water. Many places along the coastline where the Paleo-Indians once lived were soon beneath the ocean.

As the weather changed, the great herds of mammals that once thrived in the region began to disappear. Some animals, such as caribou and musk oxen, retreated north to the Arctic where it was still

When the first people arrived in the New World, great herds of mastodon, mammoth, musk ox, caribou, and other animals roamed the plains. The Indians hunted them for food. Shown here is a woolly mammoth.

9

Clay pots could often be quite elaborate. Sometimes faces representing spirits were carved onto the pot, as in the Lenape (Munsee style) pot shown here. See if you can spot the two eyes and the mouth etched just below the pot's rim.

cold and where they could survive. Other animals, such as the woolly mammoth and mastodon, died out. The plants the animals needed were also changing. The bare tundra gave way to forests of oak, chestnut, and hemlock.

As the natural resources in the area changed, different groups of Native Americans moved in and out of the New York area. Some groups who preferred their old way of life followed the retreating herds north to colder regions, while other groups moved in. Others remained just where they were and intermarried with the newcomers or fought with them.

In time, the native peoples of the northeast developed new kinds of tools and found new sources of food. About 3,000 years ago, they began to make pottery. About 1,500 years ago, they were making bows and arrows, and soon after they tended small gardens.

The exact time the Algonquians entered the New York area is unknown. Some linguists, people who study languages, believe that the ancestors of all the Algonquian groups originally lived in Canada, in the region north of the Great Lakes. These scholars speculate that about 2,500 to 3,000 years ago, the different Algonquian peoples broke away from the ancestral tribe and began migrating to their new homelands.

Archaeologists, people who dig for and study ancient remains, tell us that at least by 1,000 years ago, the Lenape, Mahican, and other groups were already living in the New York State region. Indeed, they may well have been living there many hundreds of years earlier.

# *Two*

# Algonquian Technology

Early European explorers described the Algonquians in their writings. "They are taller than we are," the Italian explorer Giovanni da Verrazano wrote in 1524. "They are a bronze color . . . the hair is long and black, and they take great pains to decorate it; the eyes are black and alert, and their manner is sweet and gentle. . . ." In this chapter you will learn about the Algonquian way of life before coming into contact with the Europeans.

## Clothing and Body Decoration

During the hot summer days, the Algonquians dressed simply. Men wore deerskin breechcloths and sometimes moccasins. Women wrapped deerskin dresses around their waists. In colder weather, both men and women wore deerskin leggings and covered themselves with skins from animals, such as beavers, raccoons, and bears.

For special occasions, they wore brightly-colored mantles, or capes, made from the feathers of turkeys and other birds. They wore necklaces, earrings, and other ornaments made from stone, bone, and purple and white shells. The Algonquians of the New York area

This photo shows a Lenape man and woman of Oklahoma in ceremonial dress. The photograph was taken by anthropologist M. R. Harrington around 1910.

called these shell beads sewan (SHEY-wun). Today, we call these beads wampum, a word derived from the New England Algonquian word *wampumpeag*, "white shell beads."

The Algonquians did not wear elaborate feather headdresses as did the Native Americans of the western plains. Instead, men wore one or two eagle feathers, which they tied to a single crest of hair they left growing at the top of their heads. The rest of their hair they generally plucked out. Sometimes men also wore a headdress made from the hair of a deer or porcupine. This type of headdress is called a roach.

Women decorated their hair with beautiful bone and stone ornaments, sometimes using the ornaments to tie their hair in a bun. Both men and women painted themselves for special occasions. They often tattooed themselves with images of animals, mythical creatures, and other designs.

# Tools

The Algonquians were skilled craftspeople. They knew how to shape rocks, wood, and clay into all the tools that they needed to survive.

Along the river banks and cliffs they collected cobblestones and other kinds of hard rocks. They chipped and hammered these rocks into whetstones, which were used to grind wood, stone or bone objects into shape, and hammerstones, which were used as hammers to make other stone tools and to crack nuts. They also made stone axes, which they lashed onto wooden handles and used to chop wood. The Lenape called such an axe a tuh-ma-HEE-kun. It is where we get the word "tomahawk."

Other stones that the Algonquians found were shaped into hoes for gardening, drills for making holes in wood and shells, and long pestles for pounding corn. Some rocks and minerals, such as quartz, chert, and flint, were especially sharp. The Native Americans carved, chipped, and flaked these stones into spear points, arrowheads, knives, and scrapers. Scrapers were used for hollowing wooden bowls, scraping the fat from deer hides, removing the bark from spear and arrow shafts, and many other things.

The Algonquian women gathered clay from the river banks and molded it into pots. Then they would dry the new pots in the sun. When the pots were completely dry, they were placed into a very hot fire to harden and become more durable.

Over the centuries, the Algonquians and their predecessors made spear points such as these in a variety of different styles. Some spear points probably also served as knives when attached to short handles.

# The Algonquian of New York

Men carved wood from maple trees or witch hazel into bows. These bows were long—sometimes as tall as a man. Arrow shafts were made from elder wood, reeds, or other straight thin woods. The Algonquians also carved wooden bowls, ladles, war clubs, handles for stone tools, and long dugout canoes.

Some tools were even made from animals. Bowstrings were made from deer sinew. Antlers were carved into knives and harpoons. Shoulder blades were made into garden hoes. Other bones were fashioned into fishhooks, arrowheads, spearpoints, and sewing needles.

This is an Algonquian wigwam, or bark house.

Even animal fat or grease was saved. The Algonquians smeared bear or raccoon fat all over their bodies to protect them from insects in the summertime, and from the frigid temperatures of winter. They rubbed the bear fat into their hair to keep it shiny.

# Homes

The Algonquians built wigwams for shelter. Some wigwams were small and round and housed a single family. Other wigwams were more oval shaped and were more than 100 feet (30.5 m) long. Many people from an extended family could live inside.

Wigwams were not difficult for the Algonquians to build. The Native Americans tied saplings together to form a frame. They covered the frame with the bark of elm, linden, or chestnut trees. Sometimes instead of using bark to build roofs, they used woven grass mats. A fireplace to cook and to keep warm was needed inside, so a hole was set into the roof to allow smoke to escape. Sleeping platforms were attached to the walls.

# Food and Cooking

Because the northeast has four full seasons, the Algonquians' food supply changed throughout the year. In the spring and fall, Algonquian men hunted migrating ducks, swans, geese and passenger pigeons. These were said to be so numerous that, as they flew together, they darkened the sky.

In the spring, the Algonquians also fished for shad, herring, striped bass, salmon, and sturgeon which were returning in the millions to breed in the Hudson River and in other rivers. They caught the fish with nets braided from hemp, a plant that grew in the thickets and fields.

Some nets were small and attached to the end of a pole. The Native Americans waded into the water and scooped out the fish, or caught them from their dugout canoes. Other nets were several hundred feet long. The top of the net was tied to pieces of wood so that it would float. The rest of the net stretched deep under water, weighed down by stones or "netsinkers" tied to the bottom of it. A net was called an uk-wa-NEE-kun. The Algonquians also caught fish with their tung-uh-MEE-kun-ah, or spears.

During the warmer months, the Algonquians living along the lower Hudson River and the seashore harvested oysters, clams, and crabs. They left huge piles of shells or middens behind—some of which can still be found to this day.

During the winter, the Algonquians hunted more than at other times of the year. The Native Americans had many methods of hunting. One way was to set fire to part of the woods. The fire would be made in the shape of a giant circle. Deer, elk, and other animals would be trapped inside the circle. That way men could shoot the deer with their bows and arrows.

The Algonquians knew that by burning a small part of the woods, they would actually be helping to protect their food supply. The burned woods created meadows where lots of young plants could

Many Algonquians believed the earth rested on the back of a giant turtle. Jasper Dankerts, a European traveler, recorded one of the earliest versions of this story. In 1679, he met a Hackensack Lenape Indian who told him what he had heard about how the world began:

*"Once a mighty ocean covered the entire world. Eventually a giant turtle swam to the surface and all the waters slowly ran off its back. The turtle supported the earth and soon the earth became dry. A seed grew up from the middle of the earth into a tall tree. Eventually, the roots of the tree sent forth a sprout, and the sprout grew into the first man. The man would have been all alone, but then the top of the tree bent over until it touched the earth Another sprout grew up from the spot that was touched. It became the first woman. From these two sprouts were formed the first man and woman, and from them all the people in the world are descended."*

grow, on which the deer and elk liked to feed. In this way the Algonquians insured that there would always be great herds of deer and elk for them to eat.

Not every hunt was a group activity. Sometimes one or two hunters went into the forest alone to trap a deer and carry it back to their families. While men went hunting and fishing, women prepared a chuh-puh-kee-HA-kun, or garden. First they broke up the earth with their stone hoes and digging sticks. Then they planted XWAS-kweem, or corn. When the corn stalks had grown about 6 inches (15.24 cm) high, women planted beans right next to the corn. The beans would grow around the corn stalks, leaning upon them for support. Women also planted squash and tobacco.

One very popular food they made was sapan. Using a wooden or stone mortar and pestle, women pounded boiled corn into a mush. Sometimes they mixed it with dried meat or fish. They ate it at almost every meal and even carried bags of it with them when they went on a journey.

In summertime, there were many wild plants that the women gathered for food: strawberries, blueberries and blackberries, wild onions and potatoes, milkweed, cattail roots, and other kinds of edible plants. Autumn was also a very busy time of year. Women collected nuts, such as chestnuts, acorns, hickory nuts, walnuts, and beechnuts. The Algonquians prepared for the cold winter season by preserving food for the winter.

The Algonquians preserved food for a long time by drying it out in the sun or smoking it over a fire. Women cut the squash into slices and hung them to dry in the sun. They tied the corn into bundles and hung them inside their wigwams to dry. They smoked fish and meat. Then they took the smoked and dried foods and placed them in pots. They buried the pots deep in the ground in storage pits where animals could not get them. The Algonquians relied on these stores when food became scarce. They also set aside some corn kernels, beans and other seeds into skin bags for safe keeping, so that next year when spring returned, they would once again be able to plant a garden.

Long wooden or stone pestles were used in wooden or stone mortars to pound corn seeds, dried meats, berries and other substances. The miniature mortar and pestle shown here were made by Charles Dean, "Red Wing."

# Three

## Other Features of Algonquian Life

The Algonquians also had a complex society, with many different facets to their government, religion, rituals, and social life.

## Government

The Algonquians of New York were not united into a single nation. Each group had its own separate villages, and each village had its own leaders. The people of different villages often traded with each other and sometimes gathered together to celebrate festivals. People usually had relatives living in other villages and were on friendly terms.

All the Algonquian tribes were organized into different groups of families. These groups are known as clans. Each clan believed that they were descended from a common ancestor. The clans were named after different animals.

The Mahicans had three such clans: the wolf, the turtle, and the bear. The Lenape clans were the wolf, the turtle, and the turkey. Unfortunately, no one recorded what the clans were on eastern Long Island, and they have been forgotten. In most of the New York area, Algonquians belonged to the clan of their mother. On eastern Long Island, Algonquians may have belonged to the clan of their father.

This carved wooden doll, a Lenape Ohtas or Doll Being, was made by the Lenape during the eighteenth century. According to Lenape belief, such dolls had to be danced around and honored each year, to safeguard the health of the families that owned them.

Clans had important purposes. A person was not permitted to marry someone from his or her own clan. This custom helped to prevent people from marrying their own relatives. Orphans were taken care of by members of the clan.

The main clan in a village appointed the KEEH-kai, or chief. He was usually a wise man from the main clan who gave his people good advice. Algonquian chiefs were not like European kings. They were not very powerful and could not do whatever they wanted. Instead, they acted with the consent of their people and the advice of tribal elders. In times of war, the chief stepped down and a special war chief temporarily became chief. The war chief did not have to be a member of the main clan in the village—only a skilled warrior who could help to protect his people.

Medicine people, or nent-pee-KEH-suk, were also very important to the village. They were skilled in making medicines from different plants and trees. Other medicine people called muh-tey-in-NEW-wuk tried to heal the sick by singing songs and praying to the spirits.

# Religious Beliefs

If you grew up as an Algonquian long ago, you would have been taught how to live in accordance with the ma-ni-TOW-uk, or spirits. The Algonquians believed that if they did not do this properly, they would not succeed with any of the other things that they did. The Algonquians believed that spirits were everywhere: in trees,

Here is one winter story told by Touching Leaves Woman, a traditional Lenape of modern times:

*Long ago there was a man named Weh-hee-xa-MOO-kes. People thought Weh-hee-xa-MOO-kes was very foolish, but he was truly the wisest man in the village. He only pretended that he wasn't intelligent but the strange things he did taught people important lessons.*

*One day some hunters said to Weh-hee-xa-MOO-kes, "We're so very hungry! We wish we had turkey dipped in grease." When the hunters returned that evening they found Weh-hee-xa-MOO-kes dipping a freshly killed turkey in a kettle of grease. It hadn't even been cooked and its feathers were still on! "Weh-hee-xa-MOO-kes!" the hunters said. "What are you doing? Why are you dipping that turkey in grease? You're supposed to clean it and cook it first!"*

*"Shey a mah lee-unt-PUN-ney!" answered Weh-hee-xa-MOO-kes. "You should have told me so! You only said you wanted turkey dipped in grease. Now you have it!"*

*The Lenape taught this story so that children would choose their words carefully. "Mean what you say," the Lenape would caution. "Words are important. They can cause much harm or they can do a lot of good and they should not be used lightly."*

Lenape traditionalist Nora Thompson Dean, also known as Touching Leaves Woman (1907-1984).

in animals, in the sun, moon, and stars. There were spirits in the winds and in each blade of grass.

Spirits were also said to live in each of the four directions. They controlled the winds and affected the weather. Lo-wa-NUN-too, the North Spirit, was responsible for winter. He covered the lands of the Algonquians with ice and snow. When icicles hung from the branches of the forest and from the doors of wigwams, the elders told children not to break them. They said that these were "winter's canes" and that if they broke those canes, the North Spirit would become angry and bring colder weather.

The Algonquians described the North Spirit as a "grandfather." The Eastern Spirit was also called a grandfather, as was the Western Spirit. Shaw-nuh-XA-wush, or "Old Lady South," was the southern spirit who sent warm breezes, and springtime and summer. She was said to be a benevolent grandmother. The Algonquians called the spirits grandfathers, grandmothers, sisters, and brothers as signs of respect.

The greatest spirit of all was the Creator. He was said to live on the highest of the twelve levels of heaven and to be watching everything in his creation. Some Algonquians called him Puh-tuh-MUH-was, "The One Who Is Prayed To." Others called him Kit-ta-ni-TOW-it, "Great Spirit," and still others Kee-shay-luh-MOO-kawng, "The One Who Created Us All By His Thoughts."

Some spirits were said to live beneath the Creator in the different levels of heaven. Among the most powerful were the

Pet-hak-ho-WAY-yok, the "thunder beings." Some Lenape groups said that the thunder beings were giant partridges or turkeys that lived in the mountains and could be heard in the distance. Others said that they looked like eagles with the heads of people, some of which were old men and others young men. These thunder beings were believed to have the ability to shoot arrows of lightning from the skies.

Gourd rattles were often used by the Lenape and other Eastern Woodlands tribes to keep time during social dances. The larger rattle in this photograph was made by Jeff Kalin. The two smaller rattles were fashioned by the late Charles Dean, "Red Wing."

The thunder beings were said to be the enemies of the great horned serpents that lived in the rivers, streams, and lakes. The Algonquians believed that these serpents sometimes attacked humans and other animals. "You better behave yourselves," mothers would tell their children, "or chee-PAX-kok, the horned serpent will get you!"

Presiding over all the trees, shrubs, and grasses, and over all the crops that grew in the gardens, was a spirit the Algonquians

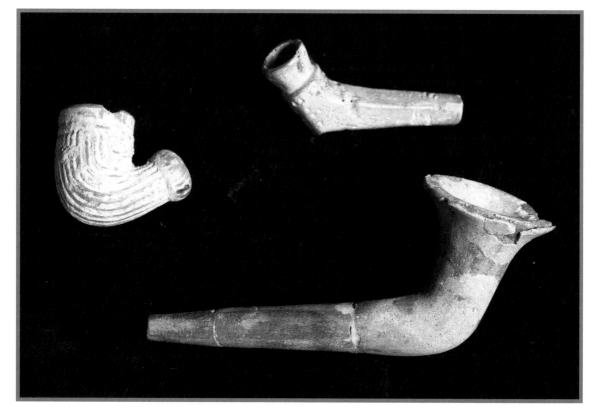

Smoking among the Lenape and other American Indian groups was generally practiced for religious purposes. Shown here at right are several types of tobacco pipes from Late Woodland times and at left a trade pipe from the colonial period.

called ga-HEH-sun-na XUSK-weem, "Our Mother Corn." The animals of the forest also had a spirit protector, Mu-SEENG-w or "Living Solid Face." Although he was good to the Native Americans, he had a frightening, bearlike appearance. In one hand, he carried a rattle made from the shell of a snapping turtle and in the other a giant wooden staff. Some said he rode about on the back of a deer guarding the animals.

Among the most important ways they showed respect to these spirits was by offering them tobacco, which was considered sacred. They also smoked tobacco in clay pipes and prayed with it.

One modern day Lenape, Arnette Timothy, explained how she learned to use tobacco while gathering herbs: "When seeking the aid of a plant or tree, I was taught to offer tobacco to the first plant of that species that I came across. Tobacco would be set down on whatever side the plant was approached. I was told to recognize that the plant was a living being, just like any other living person and therefore was to be treated with respect. You thank this plant for what it is providing you with and you tell it why you are taking its medicine."

Many rituals were performed during the lifetime of the Algonquians, from birth to the beginning of manhood or womanhood, marriage, aging, and death. The Algonquians also believed that rituals were necessary to ensure that the fish, animals, and vegetation would always return. The Algonquians had other dances and ceremonies to honor the Guardian of the Game Animals, Mother Corn spirit, and other ma-ni-TOW-uk, or spirits.

# Entertainment and Sports

The Algonquians often sang and danced just for the fun of it, and children, as well as adults, often played games. They played a game in which hollow bones were attached by a string to a pointed stick. The players tried to toss up the bones and catch them on the stick. They also played a game called hoop and spear. They threw spears through a rolling hoop to try to stop it.

A favorite game of the Algonquians was football, but the game was very different from the kind of football we play today. In Algonquian football, the boys played against the girls. A deerskin ball was used. Boys were not permitted to touch the ball and could only kick it toward the goal posts. Girls were allowed to carry the ball and to tackle the boys. Sometimes the girls even gave the ball to an old lady. None of the boys would dare to stop an old lady, and she would carry the ball all the way to the goal posts and win an easy point for the girls! After the game, people had a social dance, which lasted all night.

During the long winter nights, when the forests were covered with snow and the lakes and rivers were frozen, people gathered around the fires to keep warm. This was the time for telling the at-hee-loo-HA-ku-na, "winter stories." The Algonquians told these stories only during the winter because they believed that during the winter, the spirits described in the tales went to sleep. Because the spirits might be offended if they heard what was being told about them, winter was the safest time for stories.

Storytelling was once so important to the Algonquians that there were actually professional storytellers. These people traveled to each wigwam with their tales. In return for their stories, they received a delicious meal and sometimes a place to spend the night. The at-hee-LOO-het or "storyteller" carried a special story bag. Before beginning a story, he or she reached into that bag and pulled out an object—a bone, a feather, a carving. Each object symbolized a different story and helped to determine which story would be told.

After the arrival of Europeans and the introduction of glass beads, the Lenape and other tribes learned to fashion many beautiful beaded neckbands and bracelets, such as these.

# Four

## The Coming of the Europeans

The arrival of Europeans on the northeast coast changed the Algonquian way of life forever. In 1524, Giovanni da Verrazano, an Italian navigator sailing for the king of France, briefly entered New York harbor. The Algonquians paddled to greet him in about thirty canoes, shouting and waving for the sea captain to come ashore. Before he could do so, however, a strong wind began to blow, and Verrazano was forced to leave.

Eighty-five years later, in 1609, another explorer entered New York Bay. He was Henry Hudson, the English navigator, sailing on behalf of the Dutch East India Company. The company hired Hudson to search for a Northeast Passage—a route by water leading through North America. Nobody knew at that time if such a route actually existed. The Dutch wanted to trade with China for spices and silks, and if such a passage was discovered, it would be an easy way of getting to China.

When the Algonquians saw the Dutch ship approaching, they were astonished. Some thought it was a giant sea monster or ghost. Others thought it was a floating house of the Creator. As the giant boat came closer, they could see that it had people on it. They had hair on their faces and a lighter colored skin. They

This engraving depicts the arrival of Henry Hudson on the river that now bears his name. When Hudson first arrived, many Native Americans thought that he had been sent to them by the Creator. They could not imagine that his arrival would mark the end of their traditional way of life.

A page from the *Walam Olum* manuscript. In 1834, a French scholar, Constantine Samuel Rafinesque, claimed to have discovered a set of ancient wooden tablets covered with pictographs. Rafinesque said the tablets had come from the Lenape and told the story of how the Lenape and other Algonquians came to the New World. Although many scholars believed this document to be genuine, it has recently been proven a fraud. It was really invented by Rafinesque for fame and fortune. This photograph shows a page from Rafinesque's manuscript "copy" of the tablets. The originals, of course, never existed.

wore brightly colored clothing and had sticks that roared and killed birds in the sky. The noise sounded like thunder to the Native Americans.

Many of the Algonquians greeted Hudson as though he were a spirit. They offered him tobacco and sang to him. They smoked their pipes and gave him their best animal skins as gifts. Hudson in turn gave the Native Americans metal axe heads and hoes, knives and shiny glass beads.

Some Algonquians, however, especially those who lived closest to the seashore, did not trust Henry Hudson and his men. They had probably heard stories about earlier ships coming to the region and causing trouble. The strange men on ships sometimes kidnapped Native Americans and made them into slaves. Those kidnapped were never heard from again. Perhaps that is why some Algonquians shot arrows at Hudson's ship and killed one of his men.

In his search for a Northeast Passage, Hudson sailed his ship, the *Half Moon*, up the Hudson River as far north as present-day Albany. Along the way, he and his crew met with different Lenape and Mahican groups.

Hudson never found the fabled passage for which he was looking. However, his explorations of the river that bears his name stimulated the Dutch to claim the region for themselves. They called it New Netherland—for The Netherlands, the Dutch homeland.

# Fur Traders and Colonists in the Land of the Algonquian

After the arrival of Henry Hudson, many more Europeans came to the land of the Algonquians—a land now being called New Netherland. They never did find a northeast passage leading to China. But the wealth of animal furs that Hudson reported prompted the Dutch to start thinking about trading with the Indians for fur. Two Dutch merchants, Captain Hendrick Christiaensen and Jacob Eelckens, sailed up the Hudson River in 1613 and made the first treaty between North American Indians and Europeans. In the treaty, the Mahican permitted the captains to found a trading post on their territory. The post was built on Castle Island (near Albany) in 1614 and was called Fort Nassau. Another fort was built on Manhattan Island in 1615.

Then, in 1624, the West India Company, which had been given control of New Netherland by the Dutch government, sent the first colonists to settle in the region. Most of them went to live on Manhattan Island in 1626. They called their little town New Amsterdam. It was the beginning of the future New York City.

From the very beginning, the European newcomers had an enormous impact upon the Native Americans. Shortly after the first ships arrived, the Native Americans began to catch dreadful diseases, such as smallpox and influenza, from the Europeans.

Because these diseases were unknown in America before, the Native Americans had no resistance to them and many people died. Some scholars think that most of the Native Americans living along the northeast coast succumbed to the diseases. For example, it is estimated that about 4000 Mahicans were living in the year 1600, and that by the year 1700, only about 500 were left.

The Native Americans' involvement in what is called the fur trade changed their way of life. Furs had long been valuable in Europe. They were a symbol of wealth and importance, and people liked to wear stylish hats made from beaver fur. Because of this demand, Europe had almost no fur-bearing animals left. The furs imported from Russia were

Native Americans and colonists are shown here conducting the transaction of the sale of Manhattan Island. One of the colonists hands a scroll to a Native American man.

very expensive. So when Hudson wrote that in America he had obtained the best furs for practically no cost—for only a few knives and hatchets given to the Native Americans—more Dutch ships returned to trade with the Native Americans the very next year.

The fur trade turned the Native Americans' world upside down. In return for giving the Europeans furs, the Native Americans received metal pots, knives, axes, arrowheads, mirrors, cloth, and many other items. The new items were as valuable to the Native Americans as beaver hats were to the Europeans. Metal pots didn't chip like clay pots. Metal knives and hatchets lasted much longer than stone tools. Soon the Native Americans forgot how to fashion the crafts that they had been making for centuries. Because they were unable to make the new items themselves, they became completely dependent upon trading with the Europeans.

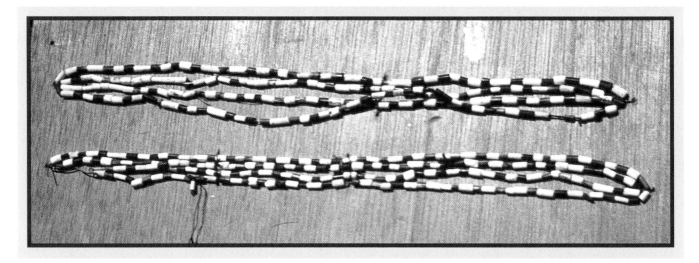

Strings of wampum (purple and white quahog shells) had important ceremonial and decorative value to Native Americans throughout the Eastern Woodlands.

The fur trade also started many conflicts among the tribes. Those tribes that delivered the most furs received the best trade items. Sometimes tribes were even able to get guns, which made them stronger than rival tribes that only had bows and arrows. When Native American trappers ran out of fur-bearing animals on their own tribal territories, they had to wander further away from home to obtain furs. Sometimes they even attacked neighboring groups to get the furs.

The Dutch were also concerned about the Native Americans running out of furs in New Netherland. If there were no more furs, the Dutch commercial venture in the New World would fail. To make sure this didn't happen, they sold guns to the Mahicans and Mohawks. They hoped that these tribes would use the guns to conquer other tribes who were selling furs to English colonists in New England and to French colonists in Canada. The Dutch—as did all the other European nations—wanted the entire fur trade to themselves.

When European colonists began to settle on Native American lands, new conflicts arose. The Native Americans and the colonists had different ideas about owning land. The colonists wanted to buy the land from the Native Americans. When they gave the Indians axes, cloth, glass beads, and other goods as payment for land, the colonists expected the Native Americans to give up their rights to the area and move away. The Native Americans, however, did not know about buying and selling land. They did not speak Dutch and at first thought that the goods were gifts the colonists gave to thank the Native Americans for allowing them to settle in their territory. Many Native Americans even expected the colonists to continue to give them gifts each year. They did not imagine that they were expected to leave.

Some colonists also tried to cheat the Native Americans when they traded with them. Some settled on their land without offering any payment and others got them drunk, then made dishonest deals with them. There were other problems, too. Sometimes the settlers' cattle roamed into the Algonquians' gardens and ate their crops. Sometimes the Algonquians killed the settlers' cattle for food. These type of incidents created bad feelings on both sides.

In the early 1640s, Governor Willem Kieft of New Netherland started a war. He hated the Native Americans and wished to destroy them. He ordered the murder of several Lenape from the Raritan band and took the brother of a chief as his prisoner. He also destroyed the Lenapes' crops. Later he tried to tax the Lenape by making them pay tributes of corn, furs, or wampum to the Dutch. When they refused to pay this tax, he ordered the massacre of more than 120 Lenapes one night while they were sleeping.

Soon the Lenape groups joined together to fight the Dutch. They burned Dutch houses and killed Dutch cattle. They fought a war that almost destroyed New Netherland. Even after peace was made several years later, New Netherland never really knew peace again. New wars with the Lenape broke out. The Dutch colony was so weakened that, in 1664, the English were able to easily take it over, renaming it New York. The Lenape, however, had also suffered greatly. In the first war alone, they had lost about a thousand lives.

Devastated by war and disease, the Algonquian villages that had once thrived in the New York region had become broken communities. Their land was also changing. The colonists needed grazing area for their cattle. They cut down the forests and established farms, destroying valuable hunting areas and valuable food resources of the Native Americans. The Algonquians were now outnumbered and disliked in their homeland by the colonists. They had become strangers in their own lands.

# The Algonquians of New York Leave Their Homeland

In the late 1600s and early 1700s, most Algonquians from the New York region began a long exodus to new areas. The remnant Lenape communities migrated from the lower Hudson Valley toward the Susquehanna and Ohio Rivers, where they joined with other Lenape who had left the Delaware River Valley. In time, all of them were called Delaware Indians even though many of them had come from New York.

In the upper Hudson Valley, the Mahican were also scattering. Some moved north to the Saint Lawrence Valley in Canada, joining with the Abenaki and becoming part of their group. Others moved westward and joined the Delaware Indians. In 1735, the largest group of Mahican moved to a town called Stockbridge on the Housatonic River in Massachusetts. These Stockbridge Indians also included remnant bands of Algonquians from New England and New York. Some had been defeated in wars with English colonists. Others had had their lands stolen.

Some of those who migrated converted to Christianity. The Stockbridge Indians were among them. They wanted to learn new skills that they would need to survive, such as reading and writing and raising farm animals. Some Lenape and Mahican who had gone west had also become Christians. They became known as the Moravian Indians because they were converts of the Moravian missionaries, people who had come from Germany in order to spread Christianity.

The journey to the Susquehanna and Ohio Rivers was not the end of the Algonquian exodus or of their troubles. Soon they were caught in the middle of several great wars. Between 1756 and 1795, the Delaware Indians and other tribes fought in the French and Indian War, Pontiac's War, the American Revolution, and in other battles.

The Delaware were often on the losing side of these conflicts. In 1756, for example, they fought against the English in the French and Indian War. They were angry at the English because the English had helped to drive them out of their homeland in the east. But when the French were defeated in 1758, the Delaware lost even more lands and had to move farther west.

The Delaware again tried to fight the English in 1763. They were led by Pontiac, an Ottawa chief. They fought this war because the English had promised that no colonists would settle on Native American lands west of the Appalachian Mountains. This promise had been broken and the Native Americans were again losing their lands. Although they fought bravely and captured many British forts, the Delaware Indians were finally defeated by

A snowbound forest on the Stockbridge-Munsee Reservation in Wisconsin, where the true "last of the Mohicans" came to settle.

Indians often adopted the non-Indian captives they acquired in war. Many of those adopted stayed among the Indians. This illustration shows a party of warriors returning captives after Colonel Henry Bouquet put an end to Pontiac's Rebellion in 1764.

Colonel Henry Bouquet. Then they were forced to give up even more land.

During the American Revolution, the Delaware first tried to stay out of the fighting. When the Continental Congress of the new United States asked them for help, they found themselves in a difficult position. Most of the other tribes around them had already joined the British. If the Delaware sided with the Americans, they would not only have to fight the British, but the other tribes as well. The Delaware Indians would be in great danger.

White Eyes, the head chief of the Delaware Nation, had a daring plan. He agreed to help the Americans on the condition that after the war was over, America would make the area where the Delaware Indians lived the fourteenth state of the union.

On September 17, 1778, White Eyes and other Delaware chiefs signed a treaty with the United States at Fort Pitt (now Pittsburgh) that made the Delaware into allies of the United States. The Delaware Indians promised to act as guides and to fight on the American side of the war. America promised to consider making the Delaware into the fourteenth state of the union. They also promised to protect the Delaware in the war and to supply them with guns, gunpowder, and other trade goods that they needed. It was the first written treaty between the new U.S. government and any Native American group.

Not long after the treaty was signed, the Delaware Indians received terrible news. White Eyes was dead. Only a few Americans knew that he had really been killed by someone and they kept this knowledge a secret. Instead, they told the Native Americans that White Eyes had died from smallpox. They were afraid that if they told the truth and if the Delaware learned that their chief had been murdered, the Delaware Indians would turn against the Americans. To this day, nobody knows who killed White Eyes.

The Delaware Indians continued to help the Americans. However, the United States was unable to provide them with the promised assistance and protection. The Delaware could not get the trade goods that they needed to avoid starvation. The American army did not have enough equipment even for themselves.

Abandoned by the Americans and facing starvation, the Delaware Indians finally joined the British. They would now be on the losing side of yet another war. Many of them died and after the war ended, they again lost more land.

# After the American Revolution

After the American Revolution, the remnants of New York's Algonquian people were scattered to the four winds. Some Lenape and Mahican found refuge in Ontario, Canada, and their descendants are still there to this day. They can be found in Ontario among the Iroquois on the Six Nations Reserve, and on the Munceytown and Moraviantown Reserves alongside the Thames River.

Lenape drummers and singers at the annual Delaware Powwow at Moraviantown, Ontario. The powwow is an important and joyful event that helps to keep alive tribal identity and traditions.

Other Lenapes traveled through Indiana, Missouri, and Kansas, and by 1867 arrived in Indian Territory, now known as the state of Oklahoma. The Indian Territory had at first been set aside as a reservation for the Delaware Indians and other groups, but the Native Americans soon lost most of this land. There were too many non-Indian settlers moving into the area and the United States wanted to make it part of the country. In 1907, Indian Territory was made into the state of Oklahoma. Many Lenape still live there today.

The Mahican of Stockbridge, Massachusetts, also had to leave their homes, even though they had fought with the colonists for American independence. They had fought bravely at the battles of Lexington, Bunker Hill, White Plains, and Barren Hill. More than half of their warriors had died in the fighting. But after the war, they found that the settlers had completely taken over their town of Stockbridge. Many of the settlers didn't like Native Americans, and the Mahican were no longer welcome in their own town.

The Mahican began leaving the area in 1783, and by 1786 had moved to a reservation in western New York that they called New Stockbridge. For a short time they prospered, but settlers again moved in. In 1828, the Mahicans had to move once again. After long journeys and many hardships, most of the Mahican eventually settled in Wisconsin on the Stockbridge-Munsee Reservation, where they can be found to this day.

The Algonquians' long journey was finally over. It had carried them thousands of miles from where they used to live. Many of the Lenape and Mahican who had gone on this journey had become Christians. Some of them had even fought in the Revolution for American independence. In the end, these Native Americans lost their lands as did most other Native Americans across America. Many Europeans simply disliked Indians, no matter what the Indians did or what they believed.

Not all the Algonquians of the New York area left their original homeland. A few Lenape and Mahican groups remained behind, as did some of the Native Americans of eastern Long Island. Most of these people were poor. Most were not accepted in colonial and early American society. Many Algonquians went into debt. They sold their remaining lands to the colonists to pay off the debt. Some became servants and went to work for the settlers. Others, especially the Algonquians of Long Island, became expert whalers and sailors. They worked for English sea captains, harpooning whales off the coasts of North America.

To make extra money, Native American women often traveled throughout the countryside, selling homemade splint baskets, wooden bowls, brooms, moccasins and beadwork. Sometimes they also sold Native American medicines.

Most of the Algonquians who remained in their homeland eventually married with non-Indians and lost their Native American identities. Others never forgot who they were. In the early 1700s, the Unquachog, Montauk, and Shinnecock tribes went to live on Native American reservations on Long Island. Their descendants are still living on Long Island today.

# Five

## The Algonquians Reclaim Their Culture

As time passed, most of the Algonquians from the New York area were living hundreds of miles from where they used to live. Soon, many even forgot where they had come from.

Because the Native Americans were now going to schools, the elders could no longer teach them the traditional ways. Customs and ceremonies were gradually being lost. The last Lenape Big House ceremony—one of the most important religious traditions—was held in Oklahoma in 1924. Many of the other ceremonies ended soon after.

The native languages were also disappearing. The last person who could speak Mahican died on the Stockbridge-Munsee Reservation in Wisconsin early in the twentieth century. The Algonquian languages of eastern Long Island went extinct much earlier, during the 1700s. And today there are only a handful of older people who can still speak Lenape.

By the early 1970s, it seemed as if much of the culture of New York's Algonquian tribes was about to be lost. A few of the Native Americans, however, were determined to preserve their culture. Among them was a Lenape elder from Oklahoma named Touching Leaves Woman. She was among the last people left who could still speak Lenape and who had been taught the ancient traditions of her people.

Philip Snake, chief of the Lenape at Moraviantown, Ontario, on a canoe trip down the nearby Thames River.

## The Algonquian of New York

Touching Leaves Woman worked with historians and linguists to record her people's language and traditions. She traveled hundreds of miles to visit with other Lenape groups to interest them in their heritage.

Then in 1972, an important meeting was held at Seton Hall University in New Jersey. Professors gave talks about the history, language, and culture of the Lenape. Hundreds of people attended to hear the talks. Touching Leaves Woman was a special guest of honor and told the crowds all about her people. "I hope that everyone will know how the Lenape did things long ago when we lived in the east," she said. "I do so want my Lenape people to be remembered." Those at the meeting were fascinated by the Lenape story and wanted to learn about their culture.

During the 1980s and 1990s, more and more people of Lenape and Mahican ancestry visited New York State. There were exhibits about the Algonquians and presentations honoring them. There were even special boat rides for them on the Hudson River so that the Native Americans could see the places where their villages had once stood and where their canoes had paddled. Some of them were so happy that they cried.

"After centuries of hardship," said Mark Peters, the chief of the Lenape at Munceytown, "it is rather incredible that we are still here . . . we the Delaware Nation are still alive."

In the pine forests of the Stockbridge-Munsee Reservation, far away from their old homeland in New York, the Mahicans are also trying to

The late Lenape traditionalist Touching Leaves Woman of Dewey, Oklahoma, makes a visit to the ancient homeland of her ancestors. She expresses her gratitude by dropping leaves of the red cedar tree into a pot of hot coals. The Lenape believe that smoke from burning cedar carries their prayers to the Creator.

preserve their culture. The Mahican language is no longer spoken, but the young people are trying to learn all about their history.

Ella Besaw was one of the last Mahican medicine women at Stockbridge. She spent many hours recording the Mahican remedies that she was taught. Today, people are studying those herbs to learn about the Mahican cures.

Recordings are being made of the Lenape language and efforts have been made to teach it to children. Young people are learning the old songs and dances. They are determined that their ancient culture will continue for many generations to come.

"Every other tribe knows who the Delawares are," said Philip Snake, the chief at Moraviantown. "But we need to know who we are. I want everything that was ever written about the Delawares to be brought here on this reserve so that anyone can go to our library and read it all."

Lila Whiteye of Moraviantown, a descendant of the famous Chief White Eyes, said, "When we were in school we were beaten for speaking our language. And it got to be so that now there are hardly any of us left who still can speak it. None of the young people can anymore. But now the children are beginning to learn it in the preschool. And one day my grandchildren came to me and said, 'Ktah-wal! I love you!' It brought tears to my eyes when I heard that. I just hope and pray that they will continue to learn. . . . Wouldn't it be nice! All those kids talking in the Delaware language, as we did when we were children."

The late Lucy Parks Blalock (Early Dawn Woman), a Lenape of Quapaw, Oklahoma, **55** holds a headpiece worn in traditional Lenape dances. Mrs. Blalock was one of the last speakers of the Delaware Language and devoted her life to teaching and preserving it.

# Timeline

| | |
|---|---|
| **10,000 B.C.E.** | Paleo-Indians are living in the New York area. As the Ice Age ends in 8000 B.C.E. and the climate begins to warm, Native Americans learn to adapt to the changing conditions. |
| **1000 C.E.** | Algonquians in the New York area begin tending small gardens. They grow corn, beans, squash, pumpkins, and tobacco. |
| **1524** | Giovanni da Verrazano, an Italian navigator sailing for Francis I of France, enters what is now New York harbor and encounters the Lenape. |
| **1609** | Henry Hudson, a British navigator sailing for the Dutch, explores the Hudson River and meets with Lenape and Mahican Indians. The following year, Amsterdam merchants send ships back to the Hudson River to trade for furs with the Native Americans. |
| **1621** | The West India Company is formed by the Dutch government and granted complete control over the territory of New Netherland. |
| **1624, 1626** | Dutch colonists establish Fort Orange on the site of what is now Albany, and New Amsterdam on Manhattan Island. |

56

| | |
|---|---|
| **1643–1664** | Repeated wars are fought between the Dutch and the Lenape. In 1664, the Dutch surrender to the English, and the Dutch colony of New Netherland becomes New York. |
| **Late 1600s– early 1700s** | Most of New York's Algonquians leave their homeland. Most Lenape and many Mahican go to the Susquehanna and Ohio Valleys. The largest group of Mahican founded the mission town of Stockbridge, Massachusetts, in 1735. |
| **1756–1758** | The Lenape in the Susquehanna and Ohio Valleys (now known as the Delaware Indians) fight on the side of the French in the French and Indian War. |
| **September 17, 1778** | The United States signs a treaty with the Delaware Indians at Fort Pitt. It is the first written treaty between the United States and a Native American tribe. |
| **1782–1828** | Many Delaware Indians and the Mahicans that had joined them settle on three reservations in southern Ontario. Other Delawares continue migrating westward. The Stockbridge Mahican leave Massachusetts for a new reservation, but by 1828 are again on the move, eventually settling in Wisconsin. |
| **1867** | The largest group of Delaware who went west arrive in Indian Territory in present-day Oklahoma. |

# Glossary and Pronunciation Guide

The Algonquian words in this book are primarily from the Munsee dialect of the Lenape Language, which was once spoken in the area that is now New York City, and throughout the lower Hudson Valley south of the Catskill Mountains. In some cases, words and traditions have been derived from speakers of the closely related Unami dialect of the Lenape language. Unami was once spoken in the southern half of New Jersey, southeastern Pennsylvania, and part of Delaware. Unami words are included in the text because the Munsee, for the most part, were converted to Christianity early in their history. As a result, they lost many of the words concerned with traditional religious beliefs, along with much native lore. The words and traditions of Unami speakers are close to, and in many cases are identical to, those of the Algonquian in the New York area.

Because the Algonquian languages have certain sounds that are not in English, scholars sometimes have to use special symbols to show how these sounds were pronounced. In the list below, whenever an "X" is used, it is to be pronounced like the guttural CH in Bach, the famous German composer.

**Algonkin** (al-GON-kin)   The name of a Native American group that lives in the Ottawa River Valley in Ontario, Canada.

**Algonquian** (al-GON-kee-an)  Any Native American group that belongs to the Algonquian language family.

**at-hee-loo-HA-kun**  A Lenape winter story—one of the stories told only during the winter. The plural is at-hee-loo-HA-ku-na.

**at-hee-LOO-het**  A Lenape storyteller.

**clan** (KLAN)  A group of families who believe that they are descended from a common ancestor.

**Delaware Indian** (DEH-la-wayr)  A name given by Europeans to the Lenape Indians.

**ga-HEH-sun-na XUSK-weem**  A Lenape phrase meaning "Our Mother Corn."

**KEEH-kai**  The Lenape word for chief.

**Kee-shay-luh-MOO-kawng**  "The One Who Created Us All By His Thoughts." A Lenape word for "god."

**Kit-ta-ni-TOW-it**  "Great Spirit." A Lenape word for "god."

**Lenape** (luh-NAH-pay)  The name of a Native American group that once lived in what is now lower New York, all of New Jersey, eastern Pennsylvania, and the northern part of Delaware.

**Mahican** (ma-HEE-kun)  The name of a Native American group that lived in the upper Hudson valley north of the Catskill Mountains and along Lake George and the southern tip of Lake Champlain.

**Mahicanituk** (ma-hee-kun-IT-tuk)  A Lenape and Mahican word meaning "Great Tidal River," sometimes used for the Hudson River.

**ma-ni-TOW** The Lenape word for spirit. The plural is ma-ni-TOW-uk.

**muh-tey-IN-new-wuk** Medicine people who would cure the sick by singing songs and praying to the spirits.

**Munsee** (MUN-see) A dialect or way of speaking the Delaware Indians' language. The Munsee dialect was once spoken in the New York City area, in the lower Hudson Valley, and in the upper Delaware Valley. The last surviving Munsee speakers live today in Moraviantown, Ontario.

**mu-SEENG-w** "Living Solid Face." A spirit which many Lenape believed was the guardian of all the game animals.

**nent-PEE-kes** The Lenape word for a person skilled in making medicines from plants and trees. The plural is nent-pee-KEH-suk.

**pet-hak-ho-WAY-yok** A Lenape word for the mythical thunder beings.

**puh-tuh-MUH-was** "The One Who Is Prayed To." A Lenape and Mahican word for "god."

**Unami** (yoo-NA-mee) A way of speaking the Delaware language, once spoken in what is now the southern half of New Jersey, southeastern Pennsylvania, and the northern part of Delaware. The last surviving Unami speakers live today in northeastern Oklahoma

**wigwam** (WIG-wam) An Algonquian bark house. The Lenape pronunciation of this Algonquian word was WEEK-wahm.

**XWAS-kweem** Lenape word for "corn."

# Resources

## BOOKS

Bierhorst, John, Ed. *The White Deer and Other Stories Told by the Lenape.* New York: William Morrow and Company, 1995.

Harrington, M.R. *The Indians of New Jersey.* New Brunswick, NJ: Rutgers University Press, 2000.

Kraft, Herbert C. *The Lenape or Delaware Indians.* South Orange, NJ: Seton Hall University Museum, 1996.

Richter, Conrad. *The Light in the Forest.* New York: Fawcett, 1995.

## ORGANIZATION

Delaware (Lenape) Tribe of Indians
Delaware Tribal Headquarters
220 N.W. Virginia Avenue
Bartlesville, OK 74003
(918) 336-5272
Web site: http://www.delawaretribeofindians.nsn.us

# WEB SITES

Due to the changing nature of Internet links, PowerKids Press has developed an online list of Web sites related to the subject of this book. This site is updated regularly. Please use this link to access the list:

www.powerkidslinks.com/lna/algonquian

# Index